GERMANY

Travel Guide Book

A Comprehensive 5-Day Travel Guide to Berlin, Germany & Unforgettable German Travel

♦ *Travel Guides to Europe Series* ♦

Passport to European Travel Guides

Eye on Life Publications

Berlin, Germany Travel Guide Book
Copyright © 2015 Passport to European Travel Guides

ISBN 10: 151875662X
ISBN 13: 978-1518756627

~

All rights reserved. No part of this book may be reproduced in any form or by any electronic or mechanical means, including information storage and retrieval systems, without permission in writing from the publisher, except by a reviewer who may quote brief passages in a review. All photos used courtesy of freeimages.com, HAAP Media Ltd., a subsidiary of Getty Images.

Other Travel Guide Books by Passport to European Travel Guides

Munich, Germany

Top 10 Travel Guide to Italy

Florence, Italy

Rome, Italy

Venice, Italy

Naples & the Amalfi Coast, Italy

Paris, France

Provence & the French Riviera, France

Top 10 Travel Guide to France

London, England

Amsterdam, Netherlands

Santorini, Greece

Greece & the Greek Islands

Barcelona, Spain

Istanbul, Turkey

Vienna, Austria

Budapest, Hungary

Prague, Czech Republic

Brussels, Belgium

"Berlin is my favourite city."
—Logan Lerman

Table of Contents

Map of Berlin..7
Introduction: How to Use This Guide........................9
City Snapshot..11
Before You Go..12
Getting in the Mood
    • What to Read...17
    • What to Watch..17

Local Tourist Information...19
About the Airports...20
How Long is the Flight?..20
Overview of Berlin, Germany....................................22
★ Insider Tips for Tourists! ★..................................23
German Phrases For Emergencies............................28
Climate and Best Times to Travel.............................32
Tours
    • Berlin By Bike..35
    • Berlin By Boat..36
    • Berlin By Bus..37
    • Berlin By Minibus or Car.................................37
    • Special Interest or Walking Tours....................38

★ 5 Days in Berlin—Itinerary! ★
    • Day 1..41
    • Day 2..45
    • Day 3..47

- Day 4..49
- Day 5..52

Best Places For Travelers on a Budget
- Bargain Berlin Sleeps........................53
- Bargain Berlin Eats............................55

Best Places For Ultimate Luxury
- Luxury Berlin Sleeps.........................57
- Luxury Berlin Eats.............................59

Berlin Nightlife
- Great Bars..60
- Great Clubs..61
- Great Live Music...............................62
- Great Theater.....................................63

Conclusion..65

About the Authors...................................66

Map of Berlin

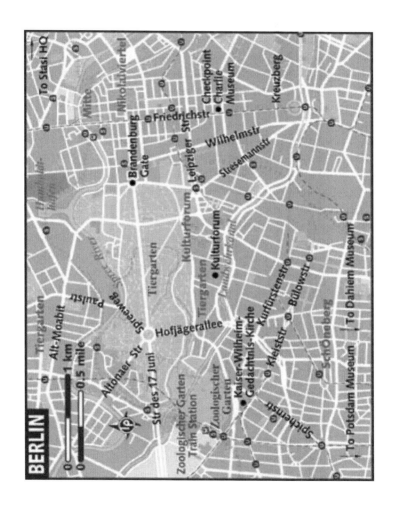

• Introduction •

Berlin, German. Here there are many world famous sites to see, like the iconic Brandenburg Gate. With world-class theatres, museums, and restaurants—and did we mention beer gardens? — you'll be hard pressed to see and do everything in just one week.

Most Germans like to plan, and we think it's always a sound idea in order to make the most of the time you'll have there.

In this 5-day guide to Berlin, you'll find a variety of our top recommendations and helpful tips to prepare you for having the best travel experience in Berlin! **Read over the insider tips** carefully and review the information on preparing for your trip. **Every traveler** has different tastes and budgets, so we've included a wide range of recommendations that include the best of everything.

You're welcome to follow our detailed **5-day itinerary** to the letter, or you can **mix and match** the activities and destinations at your own discretion.

Most importantly, we know you'll have a marvelous time in Berlin!

Enjoy!

The Passport to European Travel Guides Team

• City Snapshot •

Language: German

Local Airports: Berlin Tegel Airport (TXL) | **Schönefeld Airport** (SXF),

Currency: Euro | € | (EUR)

Country Code: 49

Emergencies: Dial 112 (all emergencies) 110 (police)

• Before You Go... •

✓ Have a Passport

If you don't already have one, you'll need to apply for a passport in your home country a good two months before you intend to travel, to avoid cutting it too close. You'll need to find a local passport agency, complete an application, take fresh photos of yourself, have at least one form of ID and pay an application fee. **If you're in a hurry**, you can usually expedite the application for a 2-3 week turnaround at an additional cost.

✓ Need a Visa?

The US State Department provides a wealth of country-specific information for American travelers, including **travel alerts and warnings**, the location of the **US embassy in each country**, and of course, **whether or not you need a visa** to travel there!
http://travel.state.gov/content/passports/english/country.html

Additionally, you may also find **German visa information** for any nationality at: http://www.germany-visa.org

✓ Healthcare

The healthcare system in Germany is first-rate. **For visitors and non-residents**, neither emergency nor non-emergency treatment is free. Visitors from outside Europe will have to pay for any medical services and are advised to purchase a traveler's insurance *before* traveling to Germany and **be aware of what is and is not covered.**

Visitors from within Europe need to carry a valid **EHIC** (European Health Insurance Card) and present it at the time of treatment.

✓ Set the Date

May - September is the high season in Berlin so it's a good idea to book your airfare, hotel accommodations, tickets, etc., well in advance if you plan to go during that time. In the **off-season** it's usually freezing (literally) and many activities such as river cruises in the evenings don't run as often or at all.

✓ Pack

- **We recommend packing only the essentials** needed for the season in which you'll be traveling. By far, the most important thing to pack is a good pair of **walking shoes** (water-resistant if you're traveling in colder months, and comfortable, light sandals or sneakers to walk good distances in warmer months).

- **Winter in Berlin** can be well below freezing. So if you're budget traveling you may get the best deals on airfare, hotel rates, etc., but you'll need to pack thermal gear and heavy coats to survive the temperatures.

- If you're planning on visiting any **cathedrals or churches in Berlin**, be sure to pack **clothes that appropriately cover** your shoulders and legs.

- We always recommend packing **hand sanitizer, sunscreen, sunglasses, a hat and umbrella or rain jacket.**

- **A backpack** can be handy during the day when you go out sightseeing and collecting souvenirs, particularly when getting on and off buses, boats, trains or trams.

- If you don't speak German, be sure to pack a good **conversational German phrase guide** to bring along with you. You'll find people a lot friendlier toward you if you don't go around assuming they speak your language.

- **Medication.** Don't forget to have enough for the duration of your trip. It's also helpful to have a **note from your physician** in case you're questioned for carrying a certain quantity.

- A simple **first aid kit** is always a good idea to have in your luggage, just in case.

- You can bring one or two **reusable shopping bags** for bringing souvenirs home.

- **Travelers from outside Europe** will need to bring along a **universal electrical plug converter** that can work for both lower and higher voltages. This way you'll be able to plug in your cell phones, tablets, curling irons, etc., during the trip.

- Be sure to **leave expensive jewels and high-priced electronics at home**. Like most major cities and tourist attractions, thieves and pickpockets abound. Avoid making yourself a target.

- **Take pictures of your travel documents and your passport** and email them to yourself before your trip. This can help in the unfortunate event they are lost or stolen.

- **Pack well,** but be sure to leave room for souvenirs!

✓ Phone Home

Before your trip, add a travel plan to your cell phone bill — they're pretty inexpensive these days and will give you peace of mind that you'll always be able to phone home if need be. You can also buy a cheap, **pre-paid local phone or phone chip** for your phone — which also gives you a local phone number. **Calling cards** are used less and less these days, but they're also an option.

Free is always the best option. Several online services and mobile applications offer free or very inexpensive ways to communicate with others from Berlin. Such services include: *Skype, Facetime, WhatsApp, Viber.*

✓ Currency Exchange

It is important to note that most bars and restaurants in Berlin do not accept credit cards — cash only. So it is important to have enough cash on hand.

Germany uses the **euro** (€) as its currency (same for most of Western and Central Europe). Check out the **currency exchange** rates prior to your trip. You can do so using **the following** or many other online currency exchange calculators, or through your bank. For the best rates, we recommend **waiting until you arrive in Berlin** to buy euros. The best way is to use your debit card to get cash at an ATM, but there are currency exchange desks in the airports.

For current exchange rates visit:
http://www.xe.com/currencyconverter

Also, make sure your bank knows you'll be traveling abroad. This way you avoid having foreign country transactions flagged and declined, which can be extremely inconvenient!

✓ Contact Your Embassy

In the unfortunate event that you should lose your passport or be victimized while away, **your country's embassy** will be able to help you. Be sure to give your itinerary and contact information to a close **friend or family member**, then also contact your embassy with your emergency contact information before you leave.

✓ Your Mail

Ask a neighbor to **check your mailbox** while you're away or visit your local post office and request a hold. **Overflowing mailboxes** are a dead giveaway that no one's home.

• Getting in the Mood •

Here are a few great books and films set in or about Berlin that we recommend you check out in preparation for your trip to this historic location!

What to Read:

Goodbye to Berlin by Christopher Isherwood is a collection of connected short stories published in 1939 and used as the basis for a famous Broadway play and the 1979 movie, Cabaret. Highly recommended!

Alone in Berlin is a 1947 novel by Hans Fallada that was translated into English in 2009. It is based on a true story and has since become very popular over the years. Inspired to fight after losing their son, a German couple begins to oppose the Nazi regime by writing postcards urging fell citizens to resist the Nazis and dropping them in people's mailboxes and stairwells. A wonderful read!

What to Watch:

The award-winning movie Good Bye Lenin! is a comedy set in East Germany during the time of the fall of the Berlin Wall. The son of a staunch socialist tries to maintain the old ways when she wakes up from a coma after the reunification.

Cabaret is a famous classic musical from the 1970's starring Lisa Minnelli and set in Berlin during the last days of the Weimar Republic, before the rise of the Nazis. If you've never seen Cabaret, you simply must catch this Academy Awarding-winning performance!

The award-winning Run Lola Run (*Lola Rennt* in German) is a fast-paced and unique 1998 film that tells the story in three "what-if " scenarios, each reaching three different conclusions. It was filmed in several locations around central Berlin and we bet you'll really enjoy this one!

• Local Tourist Information •

Berlin Tourist Information offices can be found all around the city; at the airports, in Berlin Central Station, and several other locations. You can get city maps, buy a money-saving **Berlin WelcomeCard**, and get tickets for public transit, city tours, museums, events, and lots more wonderful assistance. **Hours of operation** are typically 8:00 am - 9:00 or 10:00 pm, however it's always best to call for the most current hours of operation.

Tourist Information at Berlin Central Station:

Address: Erdgeschoss/Eingang Europaplatz, 10557, Berlin, TIERGARTEN
Phone Number: +49 (0) 30 25 00 25
E-mail: information@visitberlin.de

At Tegel Airport:

Location: Terminal A, Gate 1
Phone Number: +49 (0) 30 25 00 25

At Schönefeld Airport:

Tourist-Information Berlin-Brandenburg
Location: Terminal A - Mainhall, ground floor, right hand
Phone Number: +49 (0) 331 200 47 47

At Brandenburg Gate:

Address: Pariser Platz, südliches Torhaus 10117, Berlin, MITTE
Phone Number: +49 (0) 30 25 00 25

In TV Tower:

Address: Panoramastraße 1a 10178, Berlin, MITTE
Phone Number: +49 (0) 30 25 00 25

• About the Airports •

Currently Berlin has two major airports: **Berlin Tegel Airport** (TXL) is the major international airport located within the city limits and serves West Berlin. **Berlin Schönefeld Airport** (SXF) is the smaller of the two airports, serving East Berlin and is located on the city's southern border.

Airport websites: http://www.berlin-airport.de/en

(Both Tegel and Schönefeld airports are scheduled to merge into Berlin Brandenburg Airport set to open in 2017, and intended to become the sole commercial airport serving Berlin.)

• How Long is the Flight? •

The Flight to Berlin:

- **From New York** is approx. 8 hours

- **From Miami** is approx. 12 hours
- **From Chicago** is approx. 8.5 hours
- **From Los Angeles** is approx. 13 hours
- **From London** is approx. 2 hours
- **From Moscow** is approx. 3 hours
- **From Cape Town** is approx. 14.5 hours
- **From Hong Kong** is approx. 14.5 hours
- **From Sydney** is approx. 24 hours

• Overview of Berlin •

Berlin is the capital of Germany. Having been around since the 1100s, it is a city full of history, traditions and new beginnings. There are many historical sites related to WWII and the division and reunification of Berlin, Germany, now a world-class European locale.

The Brandenburg Gate is the iconic symbol of Berlin, not far from the Reichstag Building or the German Parliament. **Museum Island** is a designated UNESCO world heritage site and a must see for most visitors.

Now famous for it's upscale name brand shopping, **Kurfürstendamm** is the 5th Avenue or Champs-Élysées of Berlin. **Not to mention** the many **less well-known attractions** that await you in this surprisingly cosmopolitan city...not to worry, we'll be sharing all of Berlin's best secrets with you!

We know you'll enjoy the beautifully eclectic city that is Berlin — and the rewarding time it has to offer!

• Insider Tips For Tourists •

Etiquette

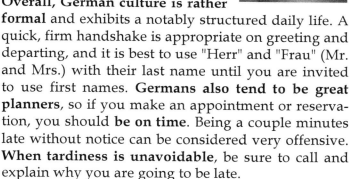

Overall, German culture is rather formal and exhibits a notably structured daily life. A quick, firm handshake is appropriate on greeting and departing, and it is best to use "Herr" and "Frau" (Mr. and Mrs.) with their last name until you are invited to use first names. **Germans also tend to be great planners,** so if you make an appointment or reservation, you should **be on time**. Being a couple minutes late without notice can be considered very offensive. **When tardiness is unavoidable**, be sure to call and explain why you are going to be late.

Notes on dining out:

• **Most restaurants**, bars, pubs, etc., DO NOT accept credit cards.

• **When restaurants are busy**, it's common to share a table with people you don't know. A table labeled "Stammtisch" means the table is reserved so you should not sit there. **When seating yourself**, be sure to first ask whether or not the seat is taken ("Ist dieser Platz noch frei?" (Is this seat free?), and don't feel obligated to converse beyond a polite "Guten Appetit." **Always bid farewell** when leaving ("Auf Wiedersehen").

• **Water is usually not included** with the meal. You are always expected to pay for it.

- **In some establishments**, it's customary for the bread and butter to be added to the bill as a separate cover charge. Ditto for some familiar US fast food chains in Germany. Unlike the US, condiments like ketchup and mustard are usually not free.

Time Zone

Berlin is in the UTC (universal time coordinated) + 1 hour time zone. There is a 6-hour time difference between New York City and Berlin, Germany (Berlin is ahead on the clock). When it is 8:00 am in New York City, it is 2:00 pm in Berlin.

Saving Time & Money

- **We highly recommend** getting the **Berlin Welcome Card.** You can purchase it in advance on-line or at any tourist information desks, including those at the airport or train station when you arrive. Admission to major attractions, discounts on tours and free access to public transit are just some of the fantastic benefits: http://www.berlin-welcomecard.de/en

- We also always recommend booking your **flight, hotel accommodations, show tickets,** transportation, etc. as far in advance as possible to avoid higher prices. And if you can help it, **avoid traveling during the peak tourism season**, between June and August.

Using Berlin's world-class public transport system can help reduce the cost of getting around. So even if you opt not to get a Berlin Welcome Card, it still is **the most economical** means of transportation for extended stays. It is safe and most times faster than traveling by car or taxi in the busy city center.

• **Eat out in the Turkish neighborhoods**. Turkish food is quite good and an enjoyable and full meal can be as little as €5.

Tipping

Wait staff in Germany are generally paid more than the US but are not reliant on tips for their salaries.

Service charges are typically included in restaurant bills, bar tabs, spa treatments, etc.

While a tip is not obligatory, it is the general practice to tip 5-10% for service and rounding up to the nearest whole number.

When You Have to Go

When you need to go to the restroom you can ask: "**Wo ist die toilette?**"

Public restrooms generally have a €.50 fee—so keep change in your pockets. You might get lucky and find one of the increasingly rare **Café Achtecks,** historic public toilets that you can use free of charge if you find one that works. Many are on a preservation list but are not maintained, so they just sit locked. They are **green octagonal-shaped buildings**. Some have been restored and repurposed as other things. (You may even find yourself buying burgers from one!)

Taxes

Value Added Tax (VAT) a consumption sales tax throughout Europe. As of this writing, the standard rate in Germany is 19%. Reduced VAT rates apply for pharmaceuticals, passenger transport, admission to cultural and entertainment events, hotels, restaurants and on foodstuffs, medical and books.

Visitors from outside Germany may be eligible for a **VAT refund** if certain criteria are met:

1) you do not live in Germany

2) you must inform the retailer you are taking the goods out of the country. You will then receive "Ausfuhrbescheinigung" (export papers) or a **Tax Free Shopping Check** with your receipt

3) As you are leaving Germany you will need to **show the unopened, unused goods** at customs and have them **in your carry-on** since your bags will already have been checked. You will receive an export certificate.

4) If you have a Tax Free Shopping Check you may be able to **get your refund at the airport** if an office is available, otherwise the export certificate must be **sent back to the vendor** for the refund.

Phone Calls

The **country code** for Germany is 49.

When calling home from Berlin, first dial 00. You will then hear a tone. Then dial the country code (1 for the U.S. and Canada, 44 for the UK, 61 for Australia, 7 for Russia, 81 for Japan, and 86 for China), then the area code without the initial 0, then the actual phone number.

To dial another local number in Berlin, simply dial the number. The area codes are 2 digits but when you are dialing another district, let's say Munich for example, you would dial 0 + the 89 area code. So from Berlin to Munich you dial: 089-234-4567.

Electricity

Electricity in Berlin, as in the rest of Europe, is at an average of **220-230 volts,** alternating at about 50 cycles per second (to compare, the U.S. averages 110 volts, alternating at about 60 cycles per second.) As discussed before, when traveling from outside Europe you will need to **bring an adapter and converter** that enable you to plug your electronics and appliances into **the sockets** they use.

Cell phone, tablet and laptop chargers are typically dual voltage, so you won't need a converter, just an adapter to be able to plug them in. Most small appliances are likely to be dual voltage, but **always dou-**

ble check when possible, especially to avoid frying hair dryers and travel irons.

In Emergencies

Emergency services are very efficient and prompt in Germany. **112 is the main emergency number** used throughout the European Union for all emergencies. Calls are answered in English, Italian, French, and German and routed to the appropriate unit.

In Berlin specifically, you may dial 110 for the police.

German Phrases For Emergencies:

Help! = Hilfe!
It's an emergency! = Es ist ein Notfall!
Help me! = Hilf mir!
Accident = der Unfall
Fire! = Feuer!
Where is a telephone? = Wo ist ein Telefon?
Quick! = Schnell!
I need a hospital. = Ich brauche ein Krankenhaus
Where is the hospital? = Wo ist das Krankenhaus?

I have diabetes. = Ich habe Diabetes.
I am allergic to... = Ich bin alergisch gegen...
There is an accident = Ein Unfall ist passiert.
Call an ambulance = Rufen Sie einen Krankenwagen (Ambulanz)

Holidays

Jan 1 — New Year's Day - National Holiday
Jan 6 — Epiphany - Common Local Holiday in some states
Feb 14 — Valentine's Day - Observance
Feb 16 — Shrove Monday - Observance
Feb 17 — Carnival/Shrove Tuesday - Observance
Feb 18 — Carnival/Ash Wednesday - Silent Day
Mar 20 — March equinox - Season
Mar 29 — Daylight Saving Time starts - Clock Change/Daylight Saving Time
Mar 29 — Palm Sunday - Observances
Apr 2 — Maundy Thursday - Silent Day

April — Good Friday – date changes from year to year - Silent Day
April — Easter Sunday - date changes from year to year - Silent Day
Apr 6 — Easter Monday - National Holiday
May 1 — May Day - National Holiday
May 10 — Mother's Day - Observances
May 14 — Ascension Day - National Holiday
May — Whit Sunday - date changes from year to year -- Silent Day
May —Whit Monday - date changes from year to year - National Holiday
Jun 21 — Sunday- June Solstice - Season
Sep 23 — September equinox - Season
Oct 3 — Day of German Unity -National Holiday
Oct 25 — Daylight Saving Time ends - Clock Change/Daylight Saving Time
Oct 31 — Halloween - Observance
Nov 11 — St. Martin's Day - Observance
Nov 15 — National Day of Mourning - Silent Day

Dec 6 — Saint Nicholas Day - Observance
Dec 22 — December Solstice - Season
Dec 24 — Christmas Eve - Silent Day
Dec 25 — Christmas Day - National Holiday
Dec 26 — Boxing Day - National Holiday
Dec 31 — New Year's Eve - Observance

Hours of Operation

It's always important to plan ahead and make sure the places you want to go will be open on any given day. **On public holidays and Sundays** in Germany, most stores and shops are closed, with the exception of some in or near train stations. Most of the museums may open, but with limited hours, and likewise for public transportation.

Supermarkets in Berlin are usually open: Mon.-Sat. 8:00 am - 8:00 pm

Department stores are typically open: Mon-Sat. 10:00 am - 8 or 9:00 pm

Banks are generally open: Mon.-Fri. 8:30 am - 4:00 pm, closed Sat. & Sun.

Money

As we mentioned, Germany's currency is the **euro** (€/ EUR) and, unlike many other countries, **credit cards are not widely accepted** in German restaurants, shops, bars and cafés. Some may accept them, but this is generally the exception.

It's best not to carry enough euros **in cash** to cover expenses, but try not to overdo it and carry too much money at any given time. In the event of loss or theft, this will minimize your damages.

It's best to utilize **ATMs** and tellers in the **non-tourist areas** of the city and be sure to use common sense and not make yourself a target for pickpockets. If anyone approaches you unexpectedly, it's best to politely keep walking.

Also, **beware the unnecessary fees.** If you're given the option to pay in dollars vs. euros when using your credit card, simply say no. Paying in dollars **will cost you more** in fees and you may or may not be informed of the additional charges at the time of the transaction.

Climate and Best Times to Travel

Berlin enjoys a temperate climate; the summers are warm but usually not above 80F, and winters are frigid and snowy with lows often below freezing.

As we mentioned, summer is the high season and can be a bit more expensive. More attractions such as evening cruises on the river are open this time of year. Also you can **pack a whole lot lighter.**

However, a trip to **Berlin during the Christmas** holidays can also be quite nice. Germany is famous for it's traditional Christmas Markets.

Transportation

Public transportation is outstanding in Berlin. With the **Welcome Berlin Card** you can ride free on most forms of public transit. A good place to start before you arrive is the Tegel Airport **website's planning tool** that allows you to type in the destination and then tells you all the alternatives for getting there from the airport:
http://www.berlin-airport.de/en/travellers-txl/to-and-from/buses-and-trains/index.php

Driving

Foreigners must be at least 18 to drive, and 21 to rent a car in Germany. Your US driver's license is valid in Germany for up to 6 months so no International Driving Permit (IDP) is needed unless you plan to stay in the country longer. If that's the case, **in the US**, AAA will provide you with one for about $10. You must also provide AAA with two passport photos.

Insurance is required and is available when you rent a car. Most driving rules are similar to the United States, however some notable differences are that officers can collect misdemeanor traffic fines at the time of writing a ticket. Also Germany has a Good Samaritan law that requires you to stop at an accident scene even if you're not directly involved.

If you are planning to drive in Germany you should do a bit more research to familiarize yourself with the traffic signs and other rules that may be different than those where you live.

• Tours •

Berlin By Bike

Berlin's infrastructure is very bicycle friendly with marked bike lanes and plenty of bicycle stands. Many Berliners get around by bike and visitors and tourists can rent them easily. Many hotels and hostels have their own bicycles for rent on site.

City Discovery's Berlin by Electric Bike - Half Day City Tour is our favorite way to see Berlin by bicycle, and it's great if it's been a while since you rode a bike! The tour lasts about 5-hours with stops at many of the major sights. Starting point is the Television Tower at 10:30 a.m. daily. It is guided in English and participants must be over 16.

Location Info:

Berlin by Electric Bike - Half Day City Tour

Phone Number: +866-988-8687
Website: http://www.city-discovery.com/berlin/tour.php?id=10980

Berlin By Boat

The Spree River rolls right through the city and this **Historical Sightseeing** tour is another of our favorite ways to experience Berlin. The cruise lasts about one hour, has a multi-lingual audio guide feature and is discounted with the Welcome Berlin Card.

Location Info:

Stern und Kreisschiffahrt: City of Berlin - Historical Sightseeing
Phone Number: +49 (0) 30 53 63 60 0
Website: http://www.sternundkreis.de/en/Cruises/City-of-Berlin/Historical-Sightseeing/K475.htm

Reederei Riedel is a family-run company that offers daily and special-themed evening cruises that includes fireworks, music, dinner and comedy; we highly recommend checking out their **special tours and events** for everything scheduled during your visit. This is one of the largest boat tour operators in Berlin with over a dozen boats departing from various locations along the river.

Location Info:

Reederei Riedel
Office Address: Nalepastrasse 10 – 16 12459, Berlin
Phone Number: +49 30 6796147 0
Main Website: http://reederei-riedel.de/en
Special Tours: https://reederei-riedel.de/en/specials

Berlin By Bus

Our favorite bus tour in Berlin is City Sightseeing's **Berlin Traditional Tour + Wall Lifestyle + Westend Tour**. This option provides a full and well-balanced experience of the entire city. The world-famous "hop-on, hop-off" option allows you to explore the places you choose and then resume the trip.

Location Info:

City Sightseeing Berlin
Phone Number: +44 (0) 1789 299 123
E-mail: info@city-sightseeing.com
Website: http://www.city-sightseeing.com/tours/germany/berlin.htm

Berlin By Minibus or Car

There are a variety of Berlin tours available but we think this one is terrifically unique! Try a **Trabi Safari**, it's arguably the best way to see Berlin! A Trabant ("Trabi" for short) is a car that was manufactured in

East Germany from the 1950s thru the 1990s but is now a rare vintage automobile.

Trabi World offers several different tours where you, or someone in your group, drives the colorfully painted car (each one is different) in a line of other participants. The trip is headed by a guide driving another vehicle and is broadcast to the radio in your vehicle. It is great fun and a most thrilling way to get familiar with Berlin!

Location Info:

Trabi Safari
Address: TrabiWorld, Zimmerstraße 97, 10117, Berlin
Phone Number: +49 30 3020 1030
Website: http://www.trabi-safari.de

Try Special Interest or Walking Tours

Experience Berlin underground!
There's actually a whole other world underneath the city. Historic WWII bunkers, cold war bomb shelters, secret passages under the wall. **Berliner Unterwelten** (or the Berlin Underworlds Association) has offered a variety of underground tours since 1999. These tours are very popular with the locals and most are in German, but many are also in English and other languages. It's important to note that the under is not handicapped accessible and and children under 7 are not allowed.

Location Info:

Berliner Unterwelten e.V.
Address: Brunnenstraße 105 (in U Gesundbrunnen) Germany 13355, Berlin
Phone Number: +49 (0) 30 499 105-17
Website: http://berliner-unterwelten.de/guided-tours.3.1.html

Explore the local's Berlin with Berlin City Tours' **Alternative Berlin Experience!** They deliver on the promise to divert from the typical tourist routes and show you the most amazing and authentic Berlin experience!

Location Info:

Berlin City Tour's Alternative Berlin Experience
E-mail: info@berlincitytours.com
Phone Number: +800 348 7902
Website: http://berlincitytours.rezgo.com/details/18283/alternative-berlin-experience

Berlin City Tours also offers an amazing **Sachsenhausen Concentration Camp Memorial Tour** that we highly recommend for a inside look at the integral role it played in the Holocaust. This is quite comprehensive and in-depth, lasting approximately 6 hours.

Location Info:

Berlin City Tours' Sachsenhausen Concentration Camp Memorial Tour

E-mail: info@berlincitytours.com
Phone Number: +800 348 7902
Website:
http://berlincitytours.rezgo.com/details/17539/sac hsenhausen-concentration-camp-memorial-tour

The German Parliament or Bundestag is the world's most visited Parliament! Various types of **guided public tours** of the historic Reichstag Building are available. You can choose a family-oriented tour, or an architectural or historic tour. The tours can last anywhere from 30 to 90 minutes. You must book at least two days in advance and we recommend booking online.

Location Info:

Bundestag Tours
Address: Platz der Republik 1, Berlin
Phone Number: +49 30 22 732 152
Website:
https://www.bundestag.de/htdocs_e/visits/besgru pp/fuehr/fuehr/245682

• 5 Days In Berlin! •

Enjoy this 5-day itinerary for a well-balanced and easy-going experience! You can modify or adjust it to your own taste! Also, be sure to **check websites or call ahead** for the most recent hours and pricing information. Enjoy!

• Day 1 •

Once you arrive at your hotel (or wherever you're staying) relax a bit, get settled and then freshen up before venturing out to begin your Berlin adventure. (It's best to arrive in the morning.)

The historic **Reichstag Building,** along with its newer support buildings, houses the **Bundestag** or **German Parliament.** We think it's a great place to start!

For one thing, should you need to ask directions on your first day in the city, this is the one place you're sure to be pointed in the right direction!

If you arrive early enough for brunch, we highly recommend having it with a view at the **Käfer DACHGARTEN RESTAURANT** in the glass dome atop the Reichstag. We recommend you make reservations a couple of days in advance, as there can be quite a long wait once you're onsite.

After your tour, you can walk a block south to Berlin's iconic **Brandenburg Gate!** (Brandenburger Tor) Once a means of division, now a symbol of unity, the facades are different on either side. It's a great experience considering the history of East and West Berlin.

If you're interested in lunch, there are many good places to eat in the area but, if you don't want to avoid tourist pricing, we recommend the **Doner Kebap Linden Grill** just west of the gate, and on the way to today's next stop.

A great way to learn more about the history of Berlin is to head three blocks west from the gate, and you'll find the **BERLIN Story MUSEUM** (formerly Historiale Berlin). A visit here is a great way to get familiar with the other sites you plan to see and perhaps use the large map onsite to choose what interests you most. The museum is closed on Mondays but is open on bank holidays and all other days of the week.

There's plenty more to see in the neighborhood, such as the **DEUTSCHES HISTORISCHES MUSEUM**, the **Französischer Dom** (French Cathedral) and **Deutscher Dom** (German Cathedral) if you're not too tired.

And this evening, we recommend a **nice gourmet dinner** at the **Fassbender & Rausch** restaurant located on the corner across from the cathedral. Not only is the food and service heavenly, high quality chocolate is used in or to garnish most dishes in fascinating ways! After dinner, head back to your hotel and have a good night's rest. Day two awaits!

Location Information:

Käfer DACHGARTEN RESTAURANT
Address: Platz der Republik 1 Berlin, Germany
Phone Number: +49 894 1680
Website: http://en.feinkost-kaefer.de/berlin

Reichstag Building (German Parliament)
Address: Platz der Republik 1, Berlin
Phone Number: +49 30 22 732 152
Website: http://www.bundestag.de/htdocs_e

Brandenburg Gate
Address: Pariser Platz, 10117, Berlin
Website: http://www.brandenburg-gate.de/eng

Doner Kebap Linden Grill
Address: Unter Den Linden, 10117, Berlin

The BERLIN Story MUSEUM
Address: Berlin Story Bunker Schöneberger str. 23a 10963, Berlin
Phone Number: +49 30 20 454 673
Website: http://www.berlinstory-museum.de/english

Fassbender & Rausch Chocolatiers am Gendarmenmarkt
Address: Charlottenstraße 60/at Mohrenstraße - 10117, Berlin
Phone Number: +49 800 030 1918
Menu: https://fassbender-rausch.de/en/chocolate-restaurant-menu
Website: https://fassbender-rausch.de/en

• Day 2 •

After a nice breakfast at your hotel, let's spend the day at the zoo! **Tiergartin** means 'animal garden' and the world-famous **Zoo Berlin** dates back to 1884 and is housed in **Tiergartin Park** which also has many special sites and memorials. No trip to Berlin is complete without a day here!

The Victory Column is in the middle of a large roundabout in the park between the **Brandenburg Gate** and the animal garden. For an entrance fee you can climb 285 steps up the steep spiral staircase to get a view of the **Soviet War Memorial** and surrounding park from the top. The **Soviet War Memorial** has wreath laying ceromonies every May, which are well attended by war veterans from the former Soviet Union. Other memorials and spots to visit include: **The Bismark Memorial, Bellevue Palace, the House of World Cultures, Beethoven-Haydyn-Mozart Memorial** among many others.

Zoo Berlin is open 365 days a year. There is a nice café where you can grab lunch. You can also piggyback the **Berlin Aquarium** for a separate entry fee, or just combine your zoo/aquarium tickets at a discounted rate, less than buying each seperately. You can check their website for information on feeding times, ticket prices and even print out a map of the grounds!

For dinner, after all that walking around, if you're hungry for some **authentic, unpretentious German home cooking,** we recommend the **Schlemmer-Pylon am Tauentzien.** Less than half a mile away from the zoo/aquarium entrance, we're sure you'll have a nice evening!

Location Information:

Zoo Berlin
Address: Hardenbergplatz 8, 10787, Berlin
Phone Number: +49 30 254 010
Zoo Website: http://www.zoo-berlin.de/en
Aquarium Website: http://www.aquarium-berlin.de/en

Schlemmer-Pylon am Tauentzien
Address: Marburger Str., 10789, Berlin
Phone Number: +49 30 218 4098

• Day 3 •

Enjoy a nice breakfast, and then head out to **Museum Island** (Museumsinsel), a UNESCO World Heritage site. It's located on the northern half of an island in the middle of the Spree River. The lower half of the island is called **Fischerinsel** (Fisher Island). Enjoy seeing Egyptian and pre-historic antiquities, and some of the most impressive art collections in the world.

For lunch today, a good choice is **Pergamonkeller** restaurant just across the water on the east side of the island. It's in the basement floor of an historic building. They serve **traditional German food** like curried wurst, a good variety of beers, and they have reasonable prices.

If you are interested in coin collections you will find specimens dating back to the first known minting in the **Bode Museum** along with **Sculpture and Byzantine art**. The **Pergamon Museum** displays full-sized ancient monumental structures created with the original pieces taken from ancient sites in Turkey and Iraq. Here you can see the **Market Gate of Miletus**, the **Gate of Ishtar** and the **Pergamon Altar**.

After visiting so many museums in one day, we recommend having dinner on a restful evening cruise on the Spree! **Book a nice boat cruise** this evening and toast the sunset over Berlin!

Location Information:

Museum Island
Address: Am Lustgarten 1, 10117, Berlin

Phone Number: +49 (0) 30 266 42 4242
Website: http://www.smb.museum/en/museums-and-institutions/museumsinsel-berlin/home.html

Pergamonkeller
Address: Am Kupfergraben 6, 10117, Berlin
Phone Number: +49 30 2062 3757

Berlin.de - River Cruises & Boat Trips
Website: https://www.berlin.de/en/tourism/rivercruises-boattrips

• Day 4 •

Today is a good day for going further a field. **Grunewald** (Greenwood) is Berlin's largest forested area. The former **Grunewald Hunting Lodge** is now a **renowned museum** that exhibits quite notable works.

The region has several lakes, so swimming and other water-related activities are encouraged. Some of the lakes have bathing areas. The most popular lake is the **Schlachtensee** because the Schlachtensee S-Bahn station next to it. There is also a nice path for jogging or walking.

At the NE end of the lake there's a swimming area and **Die Fischerhütte am Schlachtensee** fish restaurant where you can **enjoy a nice lunch**. The neighborhood around Grunewald is one of the wealthiest with upscale mansions on quiet tree-lined streets.

The S-Bahn Grunewald station is a 20-minute walk to the **Teufelssee** (lake). Here you will find **Ökowerk**, a nature conservation and ecological education center that offers activities for kids. **On weekends** there is also an **outdoor café** on site. It is also the site of Berlin's first waterworks. From Ökowerk's front entrance you can climb the 377 feet up to **Teufelsberg**, a man-made mountain that was a winter sports area in the early 1950s turned top-secret Cold War spy facility by the NSA.

There are many more things to see and do in Grunewald Forest; we've just covered the easiest to reach. For the more dauntless hikers, there is a 3-hour trek from

Teufelsberg to **Grunewaldturm** or Grunewald Tower at the **Havel River**.

If you do end up going that far, you can finish up your day at the **Restaurant Grunewaldturm** one of the top 10 beer gardens in all of Berlin. They are open year round from 10:00 am - 11:00 pm. From there you can take a 218 bus back to the Wannsee S-Bahn station to get back to your hotel. What a full day!

Location Information:

Grunewald Hunting Lodge
Address: Weg Hüttenweg 100 D - 14195, Berlin
Phone Number: +49 (0) 30 813 3597
Website: http://www.spsg.de/en/home

Die Fischerhütte am Schlachtensee
Address: Fischerhüttenstraße 136 14163, Berlin
Phone Number: +49 30 80 498 310
Website: http://www.fischerhuette-berlin.de

Naturschutzzentrum Ökowerk Berlin e.V
Address: Teufelsseechaussee 22 - 14193, Berlin
Phone Number: +49 (0) 30 30 00 050
Website: http://www.oekowerk.de/direkt-zu/karte/lage and
http://www.oekowerk.de/direkt-zu/karte/gelaendeplan

Restaurant Grunewaldturm
Address: Havelchaussee 61, 14193, Berlin-Wilmersdorf
Phone Number: +49 30 417 20 001

Website: http://www.restaurant-grunewaldturm.de

• Day 5 •

Today will simply be unforgettable! After a busy last four days, today you deserve a nice treat. We recommend capping off your stay in Berlin with none other than **Berlin City Tours'** fabulous **Palace Tour, Dinner and a Classical Concert!**

Everything kicks off with a tour of the dazzling **Charlottenburg Palace**, which includes a multi-lingual audio guide. After which you'll enjoy a **three-course gourmet meal** by candlelight at the world-famous **Orangery**, immediately followed by a **magical concert** at the **Grand Orangery** at Charlottenburg Palace. It doesn't get much better than this...we hope you enjoy!

Location Information:

Berlin City Tours | Classical Concert + Tour + Dinner
E-mail: info@berlincitytours.com
Phone Number: +800 348 7902
Website:
http://berlincitytours.rezgo.com/details/18539/Classical-Concert-Tour-Dinner

• Best Places For Travelers on a Budget •

Bargain Berlin Sleeps

The **A&O Berlin Friedrichshain** is both a hotel and hostel housed in a renovated factory building. Highly rated by customers it has over 230 rooms and is located in the center of Berlin's trendy **Friedrichshain neighborhood**. Whether you choose to stay in the dorm or a private room they're always clean and fresh. **Just a five-minute walk** to the train station, you have easy access to most of the popular attractions. The hotel has great amenities, such as an outdoor garden, bar, playroom for kids, bicycle rentals and more; all while being light on your budget.

Location Info:

A&O Berlin Friedrichshain

Address: Boxhagener Str. 73, Friedrichshain-Kreuzberg, 10245, Berlin
Phone Number: +49 (0) 30 297 781 54 00
Website: http://www.aohostels.com/en/berlin/berlin-friedrichshain

The Hotel Pension Nürnberger Eck is a bit smaller, having only eight rooms. Located in a 100-year-old building, the décor gives you a taste of a Berlin gone by. Once a residence, it has been used as a hotel since the 1920s. The "Augsburger Straße" subway station is located directly across the street for easy access!

Location Info:

Hotel Pension Nürnberger Eck
Address: Nürnberger Strasse 24A, 10789, Berlin
Phone Number: +49 30 235 17 80
Website: http://www.nuernberger-eck.de

The City Gallery Berlin Hotel has great guest feedback and low rates that compare with a youth hostel. The rooms are small but bright and cheery. The train station is five minutes away on foot, with trains running every 5 minutes, making it easy to get out and about in good time.

Location Info:

City Gallery Berlin Hotel
Address: Jenaer Strasse 2, 10717, Berlin
Phone Number: +49 (0) 30 236 2369 0

Website: http://www.hotel-city-gallery.de/default.aspx?lang=en

Bargain Berlin Eats

Burgermeister is located in a renovated Café Achteck in the Kreuzberg neighborhood. They open at 11:00 am and stay open until the wee hours of the morning. We love it here — they're the best burgers for the price in all of Berlin!

Location Info:

Burgermeister
Address: Oberbaumstrasse 8, 10997, Berlin
Phone Number: +49 30 23 883 840
Website: http://www.burger-meister.de

Rogacki is a third generation family run delicatessen in business since 1928 featuring German and international dishes, open 6 days a week. Best of all they deliver! The menus are available on their website; note that there is more than one menu tab.

Location Info:

Rogacki
Address: Wilmersdorfer Str.145/46 10585, Berlin-Charlottenburg
Phone Number: +49 (0) 30 34 382 50
Website: http://www.rogacki.de

Berlin has a large Turkish population and when you want good food at a reasonable price, the **Kreuzberg neighborhood** is one of the best. **Gel Gör Inegöl Köfteci** is a popular spot open 24 hours. Besides kofte, they offer a good selection of beers and other types of yummy Turkish cuisine.

Location Info:

Gel Gör Inegöl Köfteci
Address: Kottbusser Damm 80, Kreuzberg 10967, Berlin
Phone Number: +49 (0) 30 69 582 753

The Doner Kebap Linden Grill is an inexpensive alternative to restaurant meals. There are several of these stands around the city but the handiest one is near the Brandenburg Gate where most establishments have tourist-geared pricing. If you like lamb kebab or falafel, this is a really affordable lunch option with an average price for a meal of €5.

Location Info:

Doner Kebap Linden Grill
Address: Unter Den Linden, 10117, Berlin

• Best Places For Ultimate Luxury •

Luxury Berlin Sleeps

In the heart of the Grunewald (Green Woods) district, the **SCHLOSSHOTEL IM GRUNEWALD** offers high-class service and privacy suitable for a celebrity in a lovely, secluded setting. Housed in an elegant building that dates back to the early 1900s, you're sure to enjoy their spa, pool, gym, and designer decorated rooms with soothing heat in the marble bathroom floors.

Location Info:

SCHLOSSHOTEL IM GRUNEWALD
Address: Brahmsstrasse 10, 14193, Berlin
Phone Number: +49 (0) 30 89 58 40
Website: http://www.schlosshotelberlin.com

Adina Apartment Hotel Berlin Checkpoint Charlie is wonderful because the rooms are fully equipped apartments with kitchens. It is more of a midrange priced hotel when you consider what you get. The location is also very convenient if you plan to spend a lot of time seeing the sights in the city center. They offer one and two bedroom apartments as well as studio rooms. Restaurant, pool, sauna, Jacuzzi and gym are all available on-site.

Location Info:

Adina Apartment Hotel Berlin Checkpoint Charlie
Address: Krausenstrasse 35-36, 10117, Berlin
Phone Number: +49 30 200 7670
Website:
https://www.tfehotels.com/brands/adina-apartment-hotels/adina-apartment-hotel-berlin-checkpoint-charlie

The Regent Berlin is located in the Mitte district in the heart of the city. This five-star jewel offers a spa, a five-star restaurant and all the amenities you would expect from a top of the line, first-class accommodation. The staff is multi-lingual, the concierge service excellent, and the luxurious rooms soundproof.

Location Info:

Regent Berlin
Address: Charlottenstraße 49, 10117, Berlin
Phone Number: +49 (0) 30 20 338
Website: http://www.regenthotels.com/EN/Berlin

Luxury Berlin Eats

The FISCHERS FRITZ restaurant is located in the Regent Berlin hotel in the Mitte District. With its impressive wine menu, master chef and unique menu of delicacies, dining at this restaurant is a truly special experience.

Location Info:

FISCHERS FRITZ at Regent Berlin
Address: Charlottenstraße 49 10117, Berlin
Phone Number: +49 (0) 30 20 33 63 63
Website: http://www.fischersfritzberlin.com

If you love chocolate, **Fassbender & Rausch Chocolatiers** has a restaurant that features regular meals garnished with chocolate in assorted ways. Located in Mitte near many attractions, it could be a perfect meal for the end of a perfect day. Don't forget to visit their chocolate shop with its widespread selection of fine chocolates!

Location Info:

Fassbender & Rausch Chocolatiers am Gendarmenmarkt
Address: Charlottenstraße 60/at Mohrenstraße - 10117, Berlin
Phone Number: +49 800 030 1918
Menu: https://fassbender-rausch.de/en/chocolate-restaurant-menu
Website: https://fassbender-rausch.de/en

• Berlin Nightlife •

Great Bars in Berlin

Nightlife knows no end in Berlin, you can stay in bars and pups until dawn and beyond if you have the energy! There are plenty of unique bars and traditional beer gardens to enjoy. These are just a few of our favorites!

PraterGarten is dates back to 1837. They accept reservations for dinner at the restaurant. Often there are live events here, such as open-air theater entertainment and music.

Location Info:

PraterGarten
Address: Prenzlauer Berg Kastanienallee 7 – 9, 10435, Berlin
Phone Number: +49 30 448 56 88
Website: http://www.pratergarten.de/e/index.php

Hops and Barley is a brewery in Friedrichshain that specializes in delicious non-filtered, hand crafted beers and ciders. Brewery tours are even available during the day. They accept reservations, except during football matches.

Location Info:

Hops and Barley
Address: Wühlischstr. 22/23 10245, Berlin
Phone Number: +49 30 29 367 534
Website: http://www.hopsandbarley-berlin.de

Great Clubs in Berlin

You can dance until dawn and beyond at the **Watergate**. If you stay until dawn you can see the sun rise from the dance floor through the window that faces the river. You're screened before entry and anyone appearing intoxicated is turned away.

Location Info:

Watergate (Nightclub)
Address: FALCKENSTEINSTR. 49, 10997, Berlin
Phone Number: +49 30 61 280 394
Website: http://www.water-gate.de

The Salon Zur Wilden Renate, better known as simply 'Renate' is housed in an old multi-story apartment building. A very avant-garde environment with an outdoor garden area with a small pool, the inside is a maze of dance floors, and even a secret mini club on the top floor. There are often long lines to gain entrance to this nightclub, even in the early morning hours! It's great fun here!

Location Info:

Salon Zur Wilden Renate
Address: Alt-Stralau 70, 10245, Berlin
Phone Number: +49 (0) 30 25 041 426
Website: http://www.renate.cc

Great Live Music in Berlin

A former cinema not far from the **Spree**, the **Lido** served as stomping ground to David Bowie and Iggie Pop in the 70s, and still offers an eclectic variety of musician performances.

Location Info:

Lido
Address: Cuvrystraße 7 Kreuzberg 10997, Berlin
Phone Number: +49 (0) 30 69 566 840
Website: http://www.lido-berlin.de

Lets not forget about the opportunity to experience marvelous classical music! **The Berliner Philharmonie** is located in Tiergarten and serves up masterpieces, truly one of a kind orchestral performances.

Location Info:

Berliner Philharmonie
Address: Herbert-von-Karajan Strasse 1, 10785, Berlin
Phone Number: +49 (0) 30 25 48 80
Website: http://www.berliner-philharmoniker.de/en

The **WALDBÜHNE BERLIN** is one of the major concert venues in the city. Legends like the Rolling Stones and Barbra Streisand have played here. You can check their website to find out who may be in town during your stay!

Location Info:

WALDBÜHNE BERLIN
Address: Glockenturmstraße 1, 14053, Berlin
Phone Number: +49 30 74 737 500
Website: http://www.waldbuehne-berlin.de/english.html

Great Theatre in Berlin

The **English Theater Berlin** is dedicated to performances in English. They produce great performances in their own theatre and also in other venues around the city.

Location Info:

English Theater Berlin

Address: Fidicinstraße 40, 10965, Berlin
Box Office Phone Number: +49 (0) 30 69 11 211
Website: http://www.etberlin.de/visit/location

The Chamäleon Theater offers a really different kind of theatre, mixing acrobatics, music, dance, comedy, and drama phenomenally! Their productions are suitable for international audiences.

Location Info:

Chamäleon Theater
Address: Hackeschen Höfen Rosenthaler Straße 40/41 10178, Berlin-Mitte
Phone Number: +49 (0) 30 40 00 590
Website: https://chamaeleonberlin.com/en

• Conclusion •

Berlin, Germany is a surprisingly modern and exciting city with a rich, unique history. Whether you're interested in classic culture, museums, architecture, nightclubs, techno music, sporting events or just to have a relaxing time trying the impressive German beers at a world-famous beer garden, your time will be very well spent in this city.

So we hope you have found our guide to the polished city of Berlin helpful and wish you a safe, interesting, and fun-filled trip to Germany!

Warmest regards,

The Passport to European Travel Guides Team

Visit our Blog! Grab more of our signature guides for all your travel needs!

http://www.passporttoeuropeantravelguides.blogspot.com

★ **Join our mailing list** ★ to follow our Travel Guide Series. You'll be automatically entered for a chance to win a **$100 Visa Gift Card** in our monthly drawings! Be sure to respond to the confirmation e-mail to complete the subscription.

• About the Authors •

Passport to European Travel Guides is an eclectic team of international jet setters who know exactly what travelers and tourists want in a cut-to-the-chase, comprehensive travel guide that suits a wide range of budgets.

Our growing collection of distinguished European travel guides are guaranteed to give first-hand insight to each locale, complete with day-to-day, guided itineraries you won't want to miss!

We want our brand to be your official Passport to European Travel — one you can always count on!

Bon Voyage!

The Passport to European Travel Guides Team
http://www.passporttoeuropeantravelguides.blogspot.com

Made in the USA
Middletown, DE
09 May 2017